GREAT BATTLES AND SIEGES

HASTINGS

PHILIP SAUVAIN

ILLUSTRATIONS BY
CHRIS ROTHERO

Wayland

GREAT BATTLES

A ZOË BOOK

© 1992 Zoe Books Limited

Devised and produced by
Zoe Books Limited
15 Worthy Lane
Winchester
Hampshire SO23 7AB
England

First published in 1992 by
Wayland (Publishers) Ltd
61 Western Road, Hove
East Sussex BN3 1JD
First published in Australia by
The Macmillan Company of Australia Pty Ltd
107 Moray Street, South Melbourne
Victoria 3205, Australia

British Library Cataloguing in Publication Data

Hastings — (Great Battles & Sieges Series)
  I. Series
  942.02

  ISBN 0-7502-0624-1

Printed in Belgium
Design: Pardoe Blacker
Picture research: Sarah Staples
Illustrations: Chris Rothero

Photographic acknowledgements

The publishers wish to acknowledge, with thanks, the following photographic sources:

4t, 4b, 6 Philip Sauvain; 10 Mary Evans Picture Library; 12 Ronald Sheridan/Ancient Art and Architecture Collection; 13t Landscape Only; 13b Ronald Sheridan/Ancient Art and Architecture Collection; 14 Picturepoint; 15 Science Photo Library/Royal Greenwich Observatory; 17, 18, 22, 23 Ronald Sheridan/Ancient Art and Architecture Collection; 24 Picturepoint; 29t Landscape Only; 29b Zefa Picture Library (UK) Ltd

HASTINGS

Contents

Battle

Can you imagine what these quiet and peaceful fields looked like more than nine hundred years ago? Picture the scene early on Saturday morning, 14 October 1066. On **Telham Hill**, in the distance, are knights on horseback carrying **lances** and **javelins** (types of spear) and gaily coloured banners. One knight in particular stands out. This is Duke William of **Normandy**, the commander of the Norman army in front of you. Duke William is French, but he claims to be the rightful King of England. This is why he has landed in Sussex to fight the **Saxon** army led by King Harold.

To the sound of war trumpets, the Norman army slowly begins to move towards you across the valley. Archers armed with bows and arrows are in front, followed by foot soldiers armed with axes and spears. Behind them come the knights on horseback.

The Saxon soldiers on either side of you stiffen up. Their faces are tense as they prepare to defend King Harold and England against the Norman attack. The Battle of Hastings has begun.

In less than ten hours the fighting is over. By nightfall, the fields are covered with the bodies of dead and wounded soldiers and horses. King Harold and his brothers have been killed, and the Norman Duke William rides across the fields as if he is already the new ruler of England. The English-speaking Saxons have lost. The French-speaking Normans have won.

▼ *The scene from **Senlac Hill** today. Nine hundred years ago, the Saxon army assembled here before the Battle of Hastings. Telham Hill, where the Normans got ready to fight, is in the distance. In those days there was marshland on the right.*

▶ *The abbey at Battle in Sussex was started immediately after the Battle of Hastings in 1066. It was built by Duke William on Senlac Hill where many of the Saxon soldiers and their leader, King Harold, had fallen. Only a small part of the original abbey church can be seen today.*

HASTINGS

ENGLAND

London

Dover

WESSEX

Battle of Hastings

Hastings

Pevensey

Boulogne

FRANCE

N

W — E

S

St Valéry

English Channel

Rouen

Bayeux

NORMANDY

Mont St Michel

| 0 | 40 | 80 | 100 | kilometres |
| 0 | | 50 | | miles |

▲ *After sailing from St Valéry in Normandy, the Normans landed near Pevensey on 28 September 1066. The battle between the Normans and Saxons was fought close to Hastings on 14 October 1066.*

The Battle of Hastings changed the course of history. It made England a closer part of Europe, and for the next three hundred years, the rulers and the nobility of England spoke French, not English. Indeed, many nobles spent their lives on their French estates instead of in England.

The Norman victory changed the way in which the country was ruled. Under the Saxons, the earls were often as important as the king, but now the king was firmly in control. He governed the whole of the country, and his rule was law.

Today the village where the Battle of Hastings took place is simply called **Battle**. The town of Hastings itself is about ten kilometres (six miles) to the south-east of the battlefield. Before the battle Duke William made a promise to God that he would build an abbey if he won. He carried out his promise. In Battle Abbey the high altar of the church is said to mark the spot where King Harold was killed.

The Anglo-Saxons

England in 1066 was very different from today. Much of the country was covered in thick oak forests. The towns, called **burhs** by the Saxons, were small and well-defended. The word 'burh' still appears in place-names in Britain, as in Peterborough or Scarborough. The Saxons lived in peace, but they were always ready to go to war if necessary.

Most of England's one million people lived in the countryside, where they made a living from farming. They worked the land for the local land-owner, called a **thegn**. The thegn lived in a large wooden house surrounded by the wooden huts of the workers or **peasants**. In the centre of the village stood the church, which was sometimes built of stone but usually of wood. This is why few Saxon churches can be seen today. Wood does not last as long as stone.

▼ *Houses at the Anglo-Saxon village at West Stow in Suffolk. They were built using evidence found by archaeologists. The houses are typical of those to be seen in an early Saxon village. By 1066, many Saxon homes were more luxurious than this, although they were built mainly from wood and thatch.*

The people of Saxon England were themselves a mixture of peoples. Some were descended from the **Celts** who came to Britain in prehistoric times. Others owed their ancestry to the **Romans**, who arrived in AD 43. These invaders were followed by the blonde, blue-eyed **Angles**, Saxons and **Jutes** in about AD 450. Four hundred years later, Anglo-Saxon Britain was invaded by the **Vikings** from the northern countries of Scandinavia. The Viking leaders Cnut and Harthacnut were Kings of England between 1016 and 1042.

When Harthacnut died, the group of nobles and church leaders known as the **Witan**, or council, met to choose a new ruler. They chose Edward, son of Ethelred, who had been king before the Vikings came. Edward was a religious man, who was later called 'the Confessor'. He ruled the country for twenty-four years.

▶ *A Saxon house-carl was a ferocious opponent in battle. The huge blade on his battleaxe was 30 centimetres (1 foot) wide, and its wooden shaft was nearly as tall as a man – about 1.5 metres (5 feet) long.*

HASTINGS

Saxon Soldiers

There were two main types of Saxon soldier. The **house-carls** were a small band of about 3000 skilled soldiers who made up the king's bodyguard. They fought on foot with long, heavy battle axes. These axes could split a man in two with one blow. The house-carl swung his axe behind the left-hand shoulder so that the blow hit the enemy on his unprotected right-hand side.

The house-carls wore **hauberks** for protection. These were coats of mail (armour) made by stitching wire rings together. They were extremely heavy. They also carried long, kite-shaped shields to ward off blows from swords and to stop arrows, stones and other missiles. The house-carls were said to be the finest soldiers in Europe.

▼ *The peasant soldiers of the Saxon fyrd wore no armour and they were poorly equipped to fight a battle against heavily armed knights on horseback.*

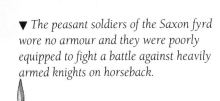

Peasants fought in the Saxon army but for only two months at a time. Each local area (called a **hundred**) had to supply soldiers, together with their weapons and food. These peasant soldiers had to fight, whether they wanted to or not. They were **conscripts**. At the end of the two months they went back to their farms. Few peasants wore armour. They fought with axes, spears and even stones which they threw from slings. The king could call on about 12 000 men of this peasant army or **fyrd**.

The Normans

The Normans came from Normandy, just across the English Channel in France. Normandy is now similar to much of southern England. There are the same trees, rivers, meadows, rounded hills and crops growing in the fields. In Norman times, however, the countryside of Normandy looked different. This was because the Normans used stone instead of wood to build their main buildings, such as castles, churches, abbeys and cathedrals. They built them, too, in a different style from that of the Saxons. Norman doors and windows were larger and they had round instead of sharply-pointed arches.

The Normans, like the Saxons, were a warlike people. They were descended from Scandinavian Vikings who invaded France in about AD 820. The name 'Norman' means Northman or **Norseman**. The Normans settled first at the mouth of the Seine River. In AD 911, Rollo, their leader, came to an agreement with the King of France, swearing an oath of loyalty to the king. In return, the Normans were allowed to keep the lands they had seized. They soon adopted French ways, speaking the same language and becoming Christians. They married French men and women. By 1066, Normandy was a very civilised land, whose people considered themselves superior to the Saxons.

▼ *Normandy was a land of huge open fields where peasants, called serfs, and villeins, cultivated the land. Much of their work was done by hand. As you can see they scattered seed from a basket to sow corn.*

HASTINGS

The Norman Army

The Normans built wooden castles on small hills called **mottes**, which they made by digging out a ditch and piling up the earth. These were used as strongpoints. The people could retreat into them if attacked. Norman fighting methods were different from Saxon ways. The Norman knights were heavily-armed soldiers who fought on horseback. They were called the **cavalry**. Knights could move much faster than a soldier could on foot. They were the medieval equivalent of the modern tank. Duke William had about 2000 of them at the Battle of Hastings in 1066.

Knights carried kite-shaped shields and wore coats of mail. These coats were split in two at the bottom to make it easier to ride a horse. The horses themselves were not protected by armour, so a knight on horseback could be brought down if his horse was killed under him. The knights' conical helmets had nose guards (**visors**) to protect the face. Knights fought with swords, **maces** (clubs) and lances or javelins.

William also had two types of foot soldiers or **men-at-arms**. Helmeted soldiers in leather armour fought with **pikes** (a type of spear). They also carried swords or small hand-axes. In addition, the Norman armies fought with archers, lightly armed men who carried bows. They fired arrows which could kill a man at a distance of 100 metres (110 yards) or more.

Some of the Norman archers may have used **crossbows**. The crossbow was a mechanical bow which fired metal bolts. The crossbowman wound up a spring and fired the bolt (called a **quarrel**) by releasing the spring.

▼ *The Norman knight on horseback was the latest idea in warfare in 1066. The Norman army also included archers. The Saxons fought on foot and had no effective way of firing missiles over a long distance.*

Normandy and England

Although they went to war in 1066, England and Normandy had had close links under the previous king, Edward the Confessor. Edward, who was born in England, was more French than English. His mother, Queen Emma, was the daughter of Richard the Fearless, Duke of Normandy. She took Edward back to Normandy when the Vikings attacked England in 1013. He was educated in France and Flanders, and did not return to England until 1041, when he was already about thirty-five years old.

EDWARDVS REX. ANGLIÆ

DIEU ET MON DROIT

▲ *King Edward was a very devout Christian in his later years. Some people believed he performed miracles. This is why he was made a Saint in 1161 and why he was called Edward the Confessor.*

Edward did not have much in common with the Saxon earls. He took advice, instead, from the Norman advisers who joined his court in England. In 1051, he made one of these advisers, his close friend Robert of Jumièges, Archbishop of Canterbury.

Edward had tried to make sure of Saxon support by marrying Edith, the daughter of Godwine, Earl of Wessex. Godwine was the most powerful man in England after the King. But in 1051 he quarrelled with Edward. The trouble began when Edward's brother-in-law, Count Eustace of Boulogne, was returning to France after a visit. Eustace's men were involved in a skirmish in Dover in which twenty people died. Edward was so annoyed that he ordered Earl Godwine to punish the people of Dover, since the town was part of Godwine's lands.

Godwine refused. There was even a threat of civil war, but when the other earls supported Edward, Godwine and his sons (who included the future King Harold), were forced to leave the country. Edward even sent his wife, Queen Edith, into a nunnery and took away all her possessions. Harold spent the winter in Ireland and raised an army there.

HASTINGS

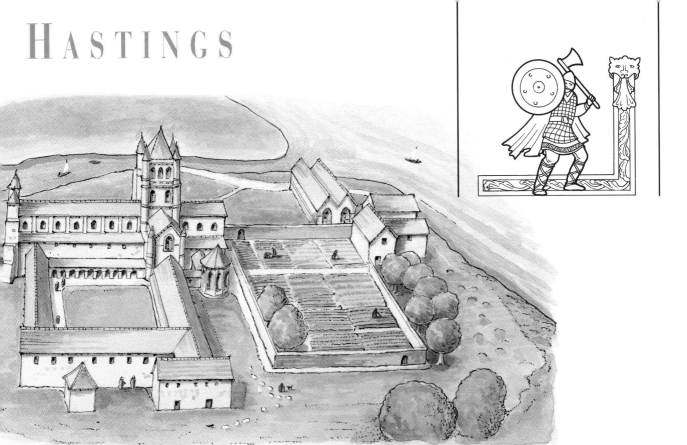

While the Godwine family was in **exile**, Duke William of Normandy travelled to England to visit his distant cousin, King Edward. Little is known of this meeting, but it seems likely that Edward promised William the throne when he died.

Earl Godwine and his son Harold returned in 1052 with the support of an army and a large fleet. Edward was forced to allow them to stay. He also took back his Queen, Edith. His Norman Archbishop of Canterbury, was replaced by a Saxon priest called Stigand. Many of Edward's other Norman advisers were also made to return to France.

When Godwine died in 1053, Harold succeeded him as Earl of Wessex. Two years later, Harold's brother Tostig became Earl of **Northumbria**. Most of England was now in the hands of the Godwine family. In 1063, Harold and Tostig increased their popularity by defeating the Welsh ruler, Gruffydd. Harold was now the obvious choice to succeed the childless Edward as England's next king.

▲ *This is what Westminster Abbey in London may have looked like shortly after the Norman Conquest. Edward the Confessor's greatest achievement was the rebuilding work he started on this famous abbey. He was buried there in 1066.*

▼ *Harold, Earl of Wessex, was very fond of hunting. By 1064 he had become the most powerful man in England.*

Harold in Normandy

There are two main sources of information about the events leading up to the Battle of Hastings. One is a needlework picture called the **Bayeux Tapestry**, which was almost certainly paid for by Duke William's half-brother, Bishop Odo of Bayeux. The other source is the chronicles written by monks at that time. One of the most useful of these accounts was written by a Norman monk, William of Poitiers. Like the Bayeux Tapestry, however, it tells the story of the battle from the Norman point of view only. Saxon monks also wrote a history, called *The Anglo-Saxon Chronicle*, but it contains no account of the important events of 1064.

According to the Norman account, Harold made a special trip to Normandy in about 1064. William of Poitiers said Edward sent Harold 'to confirm his promise by an oath.'

Harold was forced by bad weather to take refuge on the coast of Normandy, on land belonging to Count Guy of Ponthieu. Count Guy took Harold prisoner, but when Duke William heard the news, he forced Count Guy to release him. Harold was then taken to William's palace in Rouen and treated as an honoured guest.

Harold even joined William on a campaign against William's enemy, Duke Conan of Brittany. During the campaign Harold saved the lives of two soldiers who were trapped by quicksands as they approached the abbey of Mont Saint Michel. After the surrender of Duke Conan, Harold was knighted by William. This gave him the right to carry his own banner. To the Normans, this was proof enough that Harold had agreed to serve William.

▼ *Harold (centre) swearing a solemn oath of loyalty to Duke William (left). According to the Normans, Harold promised to support William's claim to the English throne. This is why the Bayeux Tapestry picture shows him touching two sacred relics at once. This was to emphasise that his promise had been made before God.*

Hastings

▼ *Mont St Michel today. A causeway connects the island to the mainland of Brittany. It was here that Harold helped to save the lives of two of William's soldiers.*

The Bayeux Tapestry is wrongly named. A tapestry is a picture which has been woven on a loom. The Bayeux Tapestry, however, is a piece of needlework. It was stitched by needlewomen who threaded coloured wools through canvas to make 58 main pictures. The work is about 70 metres (230 feet) long and 50 centimetres (20 inches) wide, and it looks like a giant strip cartoon. The needlewomen who stitched it may have been English but the designer was a Norman. He wanted to please Bishop Odo of Bayeux, Duke William's half-brother. Odo fought at Hastings himself. This is why he is shown in the tapestry carrying a mace.

▼ *Bishop Odo, as shown on the Bayeux Tapestry. Because he was a bishop he could not use a sword in battle, but he could carry a mace. Many historians think that the tapestry was ordered by Bishop Odo for the consecration of his new cathedral in Bayeux in 1077.*

The Next King of England

▲ This picture from the Bayeux Tapestry shows King Harold after his coronation in Westminster Abbey on 6 January 1066. Since he was not the king's son or heir, he was crowned in a hurry to stop other people claiming the throne before him.

Harold and William seemed to have been allies in 1064, but they soon became bitter enemies. Edward the Confessor died on 5 January 1066, leaving no children. The Saxons immediately claimed that Edward, on his deathbed, had named Harold as the next king of England. This meant that Edward had broken his promise to William, which the Normans refused to accept. Neither would they accept the decision of the Saxon Witan when it was agreed that Harold should become king. The Normans thought it extremely suspicious when Harold was quickly crowned king in Westminster Abbey. William of Poitiers said he was crowned 'on the very day of Edward's funeral, when all the people were in mourning'.

In fact, neither William nor Harold had a good claim to the throne. Harold had no royal blood; his claim rested simply on the fact that he was the most powerful man in England and had the backing of the Witan. As for William, he was only a distant cousin of the former king. A young boy, Edgar the Atheling, had a better claim than either man. Edgar was the great-grandson of Ethelred the Unready (father of Edward the Confessor), but he was too young to be king, even though he did have royal blood. Two other men also claimed the throne. They were Harold Hardrada, King of Norway, and Swein, King of Denmark. They based their claims on the fact that Cnut had been King of England as well as King of Denmark and Norway from 1028 to 1035.

HASTINGS

Harold had other problems as well. He had quarrelled with his brother Tostig who had been forced to leave the country and was now Harold's sworn enemy. The worries of the Saxons grew when they saw Halley's **comet** in the sky in April. A monk wrote that all over 'England there was seen a sign in the skies such as had never been seen before'. Many of the Saxons took the comet as a sign of a great disaster to come.

William, meanwhile, was planning an invasion. He first obtained the support of the other great rulers of Europe and also the blessing of the Pope. William called for volunteers and thousands agreed to fight for him. They were excited at the prospect of war and the promise of large estates if they won. Supporters came from Flanders, Brittany and other parts of Europe as well as from Normandy itself. They were led by some of the greatest nobles and churchmen of the time, such as Bishop Odo of Bayeux, Count Eustace of Boulogne, and the Bishop of Coutances.

Harold knew of William's plans. So when Tostig returned with a small fleet of ships and attacked a number of towns on the south coast, Harold believed that Tostig must be in league with William. This is why he called up a large navy to defend the coast. He also called up the peasant soldiers of the fyrd and stationed them along the shore.

Tostig's challenge was soon over. However, the soldiers of the fyrd had served their two months. They returned to their homes in early September, when Harold was to need them most.

▲ *Every 76 years Halley's comet can be seen in the night sky. It could be seen over England at the end of April 1066. The superstitious Saxons were afraid and thought this mysterious sign meant an invasion.*

The Normans Prepare for War

Early in 1066, William had held a **Council** of his leading men. Against the advice of some of his barons, he had decided to invade England. At that time, however, William did not have enough ships to carry his army to England. His first task, then, was to build a fleet of ships. The Bayeux Tapestry shows Norman workers cutting down trees, and using tools called planes to shape the rough wood into planks. They used hammers and other tools to put the ships together. When the ships were ready, pulleys dragged them to the shore to be launched.

The Bayeux Tapestry also shows how the Normans loaded their ships with armour, helmets, swords and other weapons. They even loaded barrels of wine as well! Most important of all, however, is the fact that they built the ships to carry the horses used by the Norman knights in battle.

When they were ready, the Normans waited for a favourable wind. They needed a wind from the south to make the journey as quickly as possible. For a month the wind blew from the north. This would have slowed down the ships laden with soldiers and made them easy to attack, since the English ships would have had the wind behind them.

▼ *The Norman shipbuilders worked hard all summer to get William's ships ready in time for the invasion.*

HASTINGS

As both the Normans and the Saxons waited for the wind to change, bad news was brought to Harold. The King of Norway, Harold Hardrada, had landed in the north of England. Hardrada had taken advantage of the very wind which was delaying the Normans. He sailed from a harbour near Bergen in Norway with a fleet of 300 ships and 10 000 men. He joined up with Tostig in Northumberland and together they sailed south and then up the Humber Estuary. On 21 September 1066, the Norsemen defeated the local Saxons and now threatened the whole of northern England.

Harold quickly marched north with his army. In only four days they covered 300 kilometres (about 180 miles). As a result, on 25 September 1066, they were able to surprise and defeat the Norsemen at the Battle of Stamford Bridge. Both Hardrada and Tostig were killed. It was said that only twenty ships were needed to take the surviving Norwegians back home to Norway. But the battle was a disaster for the Saxons as well, since a large number of their best soldiers had been killed. Also the army was now in the wrong place at the wrong time. The Normans were already landing in Sussex, 400 kilometres (240 miles) to the south.

▶ *During the autumn of 1066, Harold's army defeated the Norsemen. Then they marched south to fight the Normans.*

▼ *We can tell from the tapestry that the coats of chain mail worn by the Norman knights were heavy. As you can see, it took two men to carry each suit of armour. Notice the helmets and lances on top of the wagon taking a barrel of wine to the waiting ships.*

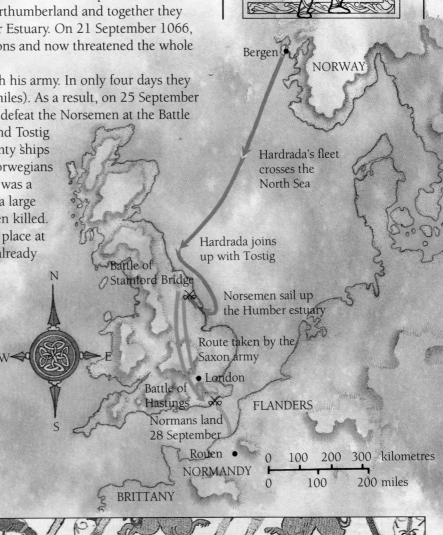

Bergen

NORWAY

Hardrada's fleet crosses the North Sea

Hardrada joins up with Tostig

Battle of Stamford Bridge

Norsemen sail up the Humber estuary

Route taken by the Saxon army

London

Battle of Hastings

FLANDERS

Normans land 28 September

Rouen

NORMANDY

BRITTANY

| 0 | 100 | 200 | 300 | kilometres |
| 0 | 100 | | 200 | miles |

...ISTI PORTANT:ARMAS: ADNAVES: ETHIC TRAHVNT:CARRVM CVM VINO:ETARMIS: +H

The Norman Landings

By a stroke of bad luck for Harold, the wind had changed while he was still in the north. On Wednesday 27 September 1066, the Norman soldiers began to board the invasion fleet. It took them all day. By nightfall, the whole of Duke William's army of about 7000 men was aboard, together with their war horses, armour and supplies. The fleet set sail from St Valéry, a small port at the mouth of the Somme River. They sailed at night with lamps fixed to the masts of the ships.

Duke William's ship was in front. By daybreak the rest of the fleet was out of sight, until a crewman reported that the masts in the distance looked like the 'trees in a forest'. By now the Norman fleet was nearing

▼ *A south wind fills the sails and the invasion fleet crosses the English Channel.*

the coast of Sussex. The Saxons, of course, were nowhere to be seen. Duke William must have breathed a sigh of relief as his ships, laden with soldiers and equipment, landed on the beach at Pevensey. The Norman soldiers built a wooden castle at Pevensey, on top of a motte. The Bayeux Tapestry shows how men with spades dug a ditch to make a small hill. They built a similar castle in Hastings, a few kilometres to the west. As they did so, other soldiers cruelly looted homes and farms in search of food and supplies.

◄ *The Norman soldiers digging the ditch to make the motte.*

18

Hastings

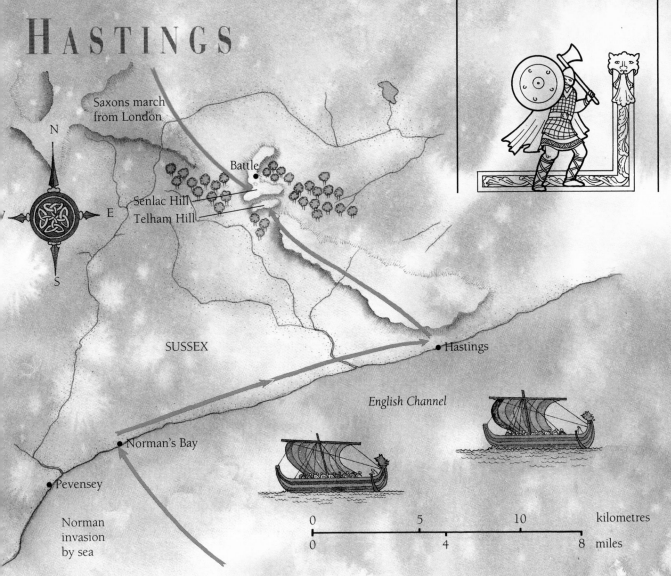

Saxons march from London

N

Battle

Senlac Hill
Telham Hill

SUSSEX

Hastings

English Channel

Norman's Bay

Pevensey

Norman invasion by sea

| 0 | | 5 | | 10 | | kilometres |
| 0 | | 4 | | 8 | | miles |

They burned the homes of the Saxons, stealing cattle, sheep and pigs. The tapestry even shows the Norman soldiers cooking food. They stewed meat in a pot, ate meat on skewers and baked bread and cakes.

News of the Norman landing reached Harold and the Saxons in York just as they were celebrating their victory over the Norsemen. Harold rushed his tired soldiers south. In his haste he left part of the army behind!

Harold reached London on 6 October and waited five days for the remainder of the army to catch up. Then on 11 October he left London for the south coast. It took just over two days to reach a point about ten kilometres (six miles) from the Norman camp in Hastings.

William, of course, sent out scouts to tell him where the Saxons were. They came back with the news that the Saxons had taken up a position on Senlac Hill. William decided to surprise them. He would attack the next day.

That night, Friday 13 October 1066, the two armies prepared for battle. According to the Norman monks, the Saxons spent it drinking while the Normans spent the time in prayer! In reality, it is much more likely that the Saxon soldiers fell asleep as soon as their heads touched the ground.

▲ *As the Norman soldiers marched from Pevensey to Hastings, they burned Saxon farms, seized crops and took farm animals for food. We know this because it was all recorded in the pictures embroidered on the Bayeux Tapestry.*

On Senlac Hill

At dawn on Saturday 14 October 1066, the Norman soldiers began to assemble on Telham Hill opposite the Saxon soldiers on Senlac Hill. The Normans had been on the move since before dawn. William wanted to surprise the Saxons and catch them off guard before fresh troops could reach them.

William could see that Harold had chosen the site of the battlefield well. The Saxon soldiers stood on a ridge above the valley. To their right were marshes, while to their left was an area of thick forest. This meant the Norman knights would have to ride across the middle of the valley. There they would be clearly seen and exposed to the Saxon missiles. Then they would have to climb up the slope towards the ridge where Harold and the Saxons were waiting with their battleaxes and swords.

Harold himself stood on the site where Battle Abbey stands today. He was surrounded by his house-carls who were well protected in their chain mail armour. They put their long, kite-shaped shields close together to form a formidable wall of steel against the Norman arrows and spears. To either side stood the peasant soldiers of the fyrd. The sight of the Saxon army massed on top of the ridge must have given the Norman knights good reason to fear what might happen when they charged uphill.

▼ *A view of the battlefield, as the armies position themselves. The Normans are in the foreground with the Saxons on the ridge. Fighting a battle in 1066 was very different from fighting a battle today. The commander had to be in the thick of the fighting himself to shout commands and issue orders. This why so many medieval battles ended with the death of the king or a great prince.*

HASTINGS

Duke William realised this. He spoke to his troops. 'Now is the time for you to show your strength, and the courage that is yours,' he said. 'You fight not only for victory but also for survival.' Then he placed his soldiers in three ranks.

He put his archers in front. They had two main disadvantages at Hastings. In the first place, they wore little armour, and secondly, they carried only a few arrows. Usually in battle they were able to use the enemy's arrows as well as their own. But the Saxons had no archers. This meant that the Norman archers would soon run out of missiles to fire.

In the second rank William put his heavily armed foot soldiers. They wore hauberks and helmets and carried shields for protection. They were armed with pikes, swords and small hand axes.

Last came the knights in chain mail and armed with swords and javelins. William rode among them himself, showing great courage. It gave him a good position from which to give orders either by signal or by voice.

Like the Saxon army, the Norman troops also divided into three wings. The Breton soldiers led by Count Alan of Brittany were on the left. The French and Flemish soldiers were on the right, led by Count Eustace of Boulogne. Duke William and the Normans were in the middle.

The Battle Begins

The battle began at about 9 am, when the Normans advanced up the slope towards the Saxon lines. When the Norman archers were about a hundred metres (110 yards) away, they fired their arrows. Firing uphill meant that many of the arrows aimed at the Saxons went straight over their heads. After the archers had fired their arrows, the Norman foot soldiers took their place. They fought with swords, small axes and pikes. But they were also at a disadvantage, because they had to fight uphill. The Saxons had no problem forcing them back.

▲ *The charge of the Norman knights against the wall of steel made by the shields of the Saxon house-carls. At the Battle of Hastings, although the knights were mounted on horse-back, they had to charge uphill in full view of the enemy. If the horse in front stumbled, the knight could be thrown off his horse. Anyone on the ground would be trampled to death.*

Then came the first charge by the Norman knights, who rode steadily towards the Saxon line, hoping it would give way. Again the Normans had little success. By now the battlefield was filled with the sound of steel striking steel, galloping hooves and the screams of dying men and horses. The Normans made little progress. In fact, their own line began to weaken. Some of the foot soldiers and knights from Brittany (on the left wing) had been thrown into confusion by the fury of the Saxon defence. They turned and fled. As they did so, they collided with the soldiers coming up behind them. Seeing this, some of the Saxons left their strong position on the hill and chased after the retreating Normans. Had they not done so, the battle might have had a very different outcome.

The retreat alarmed the Norman leaders. It looked as if the Norman army might be in danger of defeat. The Bayeux Tapestry shows knights and horses in confusion. Some of the horses have been killed and their unhorsed riders stagger around the battlefield.

HASTINGS

◄ *The Bayeux Tapestry shows vividly the confusion in the Norman ranks.*

In the midst of all this chaos, Duke William either fell off his mount or his horse was killed under him. It was enough to cause a rumour to spread quickly through the ranks of the Norman soldiers. Duke William has fallen! The Duke is dead! To a soldier in the Norman army this was disastrous news. The battle was being fought to put the Duke on the English throne. If he was dead, what was the point of going on?

William must have realised this at once. He quickly mounted another horse and took action to stop the panic. Then he did a brave thing. He took off his helmet while the battle was still raging. Raising his head, he shouted out to his troops, 'Look at me well, I am still alive and by the grace of God I shall yet prove victor'.

▼ *Duke William took a great risk when he removed his helmet during the battle. He could have been killed by a spear or stone hurled by a Saxon peasant.*

A Norman Victory

William's action put fresh heart into his troops. They closed in on the Saxon soldiers who had broken ranks to chase the Normans and soon cut them down. The Saxons had by now lost the protection given by the slope. They were surrounded on all sides by soldiers with better weapons and better armour.

William of Poitiers said the Normans later trapped the Saxons into breaking ranks. Twice they chased Norman soldiers down the hill, and twice they were cut to pieces.

Slowly, the Normans with their better weapons, their archers and their knights on horseback began to win the battle. At dusk the Saxons could see that their cause was lost. When the Saxon soldiers learned that Harold, his brothers, and many other great Saxon earls and thegns had been killed, they fled as rapidly as they could. By now the ground was covered with corpses and soaking in blood. Many wounded men on the ground 'were trampled to death under the hooves of runaway horses'. Those who were lucky got away as best they could. Some of the retreating Saxons, however continued to fight. They took advantage of the steep ground behind the battlefield to ambush the Normans who pursued them.

▼ *This famous scene from the Bayeux Tapestry led many people in the past to think that Harold was the soldier on the left, who was killed when an archer shot an arrow in his eye. Today people think Harold is the soldier on the right being killed by the horseman's sword.*

▶ *Duke William and the Norman army won the Battle of Hastings because they were better armed than the Saxon soldiers. In the end, the Saxon housecarls were no match for armed knights on horseback.*

HASTINGS

When the battle was at last over, Duke William returned to the battlefield. William of Poitiers said, 'he could not gaze without pity' on all the bloodshed. The 'bloodstained battle-ground was covered with the pick of the young men and nobility of England'.

It is not certain how Harold died. People used to think he was killed when Norman soldiers fired a volley of arrows into the air and one of them pierced his eye. This legend came about because at the end of the Bayeux Tapestry, a picture seems to show a soldier tugging at an arrow in his eye. Above the picture are the **Latin** words *HIC HAROLD REX INTERFECTUS EST*, which means, *HERE KING HAROLD HAS BEEN KILLED*.

In fact, the soldier in the picture does not even appear to be wounded. He stands upright, and a close look shows that the arrow is not actually in his eye. In any case, if he had been killed, he would have been shown falling to the ground. This is why most people now think that Harold is the man on the right with the battleaxe. He has been struck down by a blow from the Norman knight on horseback. It seems more likely, therefore, that Harold was killed by a blow from a sword.

The Norman Conquest

After the battle, William returned to Hastings. He waited for the English to accept him as their king, and when they failed to do so, he marched on London. William's soldiers destroyed buildings and crops as they made their way to the city, to show their lord's displeasure. This is why the leading men of London came out to meet him before he could destroy their city. They surrendered to William and swore they would be loyal. William took **hostages**, people who would be put to death if the Londoners broke their promises.

On Christmas Day, 1066, William was crowned king in Westminster Abbey. During the ceremony, the crowds inside the Abbey shouted their loyalty to the king in French and in English. This alarmed the Norman soldiers outside the Abbey, who thought there had been an attempt on the life of the king. In their alarm, they set fire to houses nearby and started a panic among the Saxons. But this lack of understanding between French and English ways was only the first of William's problems. William had still to subdue the rest of England. Yet his small army of Normans was much smaller than the million or more Saxons who lived in England at that time. There was another problem, too. Few of the Normans spoke English while few of the Saxons spoke French.

William started in the west of England in 1067. Then he marched north and built castles at Nottingham, York, and Lincoln. In 1068 he had to quell a rebellion in Yorkshire and Northumberland, following which he fought off a challenge from Harold's sons who had sailed from Ireland. In 1069 there came a fresh challenge. This time it was from the sons of King Swein of Denmark.

▲ *The first Norman castles were built in a hurry. They were made of wood and erected on a motte. A wooden fence was built around the motte to form a large enclosure called a bailey.*

HASTINGS

Once again the people of the north joined a rebellion against Norman rule. Once again William had to march north. This time he laid waste much of Yorkshire, burning fields and buildings. He crushed the rebellion and by 1071, he was firmly in control. The Norman Conquest of England had been completed.

The Baron's Reward

William gave away most of the estates which had belonged to the Saxon thegns to his barons, as their reward for fighting at Hastings. In return the barons swore to be faithful to him. They also agreed to supply knights when the king needed them. Some of these new estates were huge, so the barons divided them into smaller estates. They gave these to the knights who fought for them. Many large estates were also given to the Church so that the money earned from rents could be used to build and support great abbeys and cathedrals.

▼ *As William's soldiers marched through Yorkshire in 1069, they destroyed villages, farms and fields wherever they went. The damage they caused was so bad, some places took years to recover.*

27

Norman Britain

The Norman Conquest changed the way of life of the people of England. It later changed the lives of the people of Scotland, Wales and Ireland as well. William made the Saxons pay heavy taxes. In 1086, he sent his officers to every part of his kingdom to write down who owned the land and how much everyone owed in taxes. This record was called the **Domesday Book**. It tells us about the lives of the people of Norman England. It even tells how many cows and ploughs they owned.

At first William and the Norman barons built a large number of wooden castles like the one you can see on page 26. They built them on top of the earth dug out of the ditch which surrounded them. They used them as strongholds from which to control the local people. Stronger stone castles, such as the Tower of London, were built later on.

The Normans also built many great cathedrals and churches, such as the cathedrals in Norwich, Winchester and Durham. The round arches on their doors and windows were like the round arches built by the Romans a thousand years earlier, so the style was called **Romanesque**. Today it is often simply called 'Norman'.

The Normans also built great abbeys. Some of these, called priories, formed part of a cathedral. Others, like many of those built by the **Cistercian** monks, were built in the countryside. These abbeys had schools and hospitals in which nuns and monks helped the ordinary people.

▼ Cistercian abbeys were built to the same plan. The dormitory where the monks or nuns slept, the refectory where they ate, and the chapter house where they attended meetings, were built around the sides of a square called the cloisters.

Hastings

◄ *The Norman cathedral at Durham was built on a hill surrounded on three sides by a bend in the River Wear. On the fourth side stood Durham Castle.*

▼ *The Tower of London was one of the first of the stone castles to be built by the Normans. William built it to impress the people of England's largest city. The Tower also helped to guard the city against attack from warships sailing up the River Thames.*

The Normans also built new towns. Trade, especially the wool trade, grew between ports in England and places in Europe, bringing wealth to England.

The Norman kings seized some of the large forests, which they turned into their own private hunting grounds. The peasants, who could no longer catch wild birds and animals for meat, hated the king for this. Those who were caught killing animals were brutally punished. Many Saxons lived in the forests as outlaws.

The French influence was everywhere. William appointed Norman abbots to abbeys and Norman bishops to cathedrals, instead of Saxons. French became the everyday language used by the king and the people at his court. This could have meant the end of English as a language. There were, however, many more Saxons than Normans, and most people continued to speak English at home. However, it took hundreds of years before English again became the language of the government in England.

Above all, the Normans made England into a powerful kingdom. Never again would it be invaded. The Battle of Hastings was the last time an army from outside the island of Britain defeated an English army on English soil.

Glossary

Angles: warriors from Denmark who settled in England in about AD 450. They gave their name to England -- the land of the Angles

Battle: the name of the Sussex village where the Battle of Hastings was fought in 1066

Bayeux Tapestry: a long strip of needlework which was probably stitched by English needlewomen after the Norman Conquest

burh: the Saxon name for a fortified town. This is why many English towns are called *burgh* or *borough* today, such as Bamburgh, Middlesbrough, Peterborough and Scarborough

cavalry: soldiers who fight on horseback

Celts: prehistoric people who originally came from Europe

Cistercians: a group of monks who built a monastery at Cîteaux in France. Their way of life, or rule, was followed by many others, e.g. Cistercian monasteries at Fountains and Rievaulx in Yorkshire

comet: a type of star travelling round the sun which can be seen from Earth at regular intervals

conscripts: soldiers who are forced to join an army, whether they want to or not

Council: a group of leading nobles, bishops and abbots who advised the Norman kings

crossbow: a metal bow which used a spring to fire a metal bolt

Domesday Book: William's record of England in 1086. The old English word *dome* means 'judgement'

exile: having to stay away from one's own country

fyrd: Saxon peasant soldiers who had to serve in the army for a period of up to two months

hauberk: a coat of armour made from wire rings

hostages: people kept as prisoners to make sure that the enemy carries out a promise

house-carl: a highly trained Saxon soldier who acted as a bodyguard

hundred: a part of a county

javelin: a spear thrown by soldiers; used by Norman cavalry

Jutes: people from Jutland in Denmark who settled in England in about AD 450

lance: a type of spear used by a knight on horseback

Latin: the language of the Romans which was used in Church and in legal documents in the Middle Ages

mace: a type of club often carried by a knight on horseback

men-at-arms: foot soldiers

motte: a small hill made by digging a round ditch and throwing the earth into the middle. Used by the Normans as a strongpoint on which to build a wooden castle

Normandy: a region of France immediately opposite the coast of south-eastern England

Norseman: another name for a Viking

Northumbria: a region of England in the north-east

peasants: people who worked on the land. They held their land (rented) from the thegn who in turn held land from a noble, the Church or the king

pike: a long wooden pole, with a sharp metal point at one end. Pikes were used as weapons by the Normans

quarrel: a metal bolt fired from a crossbow

Romanesque: a style of architecture used by the Normans. So named because of the round arches which were built like those of the Romans

Romans: people from central Italy who gradually conquered and ruled land around the Mediterranean Sea as well as Britain

Saxons: people living in England in 1066 who came originally from Saxony in Germany

Senlac Hill: the low ridge occupied by the Saxon soldiers at the Battle of Hastings

Telham Hill: the hill occupied by the Norman soldiers at the start of the Battle of Hastings

Hastings

thegn: a Saxon noble

Vikings: the name given to the warlike people of Scandinavia about a thousand years ago

visor: a flap on a knight's helmet with slits for eyes. It protected the face

Wessex: the most powerful earldom in England

Witan: a council of nobles and church leaders who advised the Saxon kings and chose their successors. The word means 'wise men'

Further Reading

A Castle, by Philip Sauvain (Macmillan Education)

A Norman Baron, by Miriam Moss (Wayland)

Medieval Castles, by Brian Adams (Franklin Watts)

Norman Britain, by Henry Loyn and Alan Sorrell (Lutterworth Press)

Norman Britain, by Tony Triggs (Wayland)

Norman Castles, by Graham Rickard (Wayland)

The Norman Invaders, by Jill Honnywill (Collins Educational)

MORE ADVANCED BOOKS

Battles in Britain 1066-1547, by William Seymour (Sidgwick and Jackson)

The Age of Chivalry, edited by Kenneth M. Setton (National Geographic)

The Anglo-Saxons, edited by James Campbell (Phaidon)

The Bayeux Tapestry, edited by C.H. Gibbs-Smith (Phaidon)

The Bayeux Tapestry, edited by Sir Frank Stenton (Phaidon)

GREAT BATTLES

Index

PRINTED IN BELGIUM BY

proost
INTERNATIONAL BOOK PRODUCTION